Contents

Contents

Meeting Special Needs of Children

AIMS OF THE PROGRAM

In any class, one or more students may be unable to play and perform basic motor skills effectively. If these students can't play, run, jump, and throw at an early age, they may be slow to develop essential motor skills as well as other basic learnings and social skills—or not develop them at all.

Play is a child's way of learning and integrating skills that will be used throughout life. Through play, children come to understand the world about them. Through play, children learn to move and move to learn. And as children gain play and motor skills, their feelings of self-worth and their positive self-images grow.

Most children learn to play and move through the activities of childhood. They learn by interacting with the environment and with their brothers and sisters and their peers. Handicapped children and other children with special needs often lack the opportunities to play with their peers. These children do not develop play and motor skills on their own. They need a structured, sequential curriculum to interact with their peers, gain feelings of self-worth, and achieve success—and the sooner these children can begin such a program, the better.

This Play and Motor Skills Activities Series presents a program of effective instruction strategies through which all children can achieve success in the general physical education program. It is not a pull-out program (that is, the child is not pulled out for therapy or special tutorial assistance); it is not a fix-it program (that is, the child is not segregated until all deficits are remediated). It is a positive program for each child to succeed in a play-and-motor-skills activity program. It is designed to help you, the teacher, set up sequential curricula, plan each child's instructional program, and teach effectively so that each child progresses toward desired learning outcomes.

Three Major Aims of the Program

1. To enable each child to perform basic play and motor skills at the level of his or her abilities;

2. To help each child use these skills in play and daily living activities to maximize his or her health, growth, and development, as well as joy in movement; and

3. To enhance each child's feelings of self-worth and self-confidence as a learner while moving to learn and learning to move.

BOOKS IN THE SERIES

There are eight books in this Play and Motor Skills Activities Series for preprimary through early primary grades, ages 3–7 years.

1. Locomotor Activities
2. Ball-Handling Activities
3. Stunts and Tumbling Activities
4. Health and Fitness Activities
5. Rhythmic Activities
6. Body Management Activities
7. Play Activities
8. Planning for Teaching

The seven activities books are designed to help teachers of children with handicaps and other special-needs children. Each book provides sequential curricula by skill levels. Each book is complete within its cover: sequential skills and teaching activities, games, action words, and checklists for the class's record of progress in each skill and an Individual Record of Progress (IRP) report.

Book 8, *Planning for Teaching,* is an essential companion to each of the seven activities books because it presents not only the steps for planning a teaching unit and providing for individual differences in each lesson, but it also includes a guide to incorporating social skills into units and lessons and also outlines a Home Activities Program. These two guides are particularly important for children with special needs. Because they often have limited opportunities to interact with their peers, these children need planned, sequential learning experiences to develop socially acceptable behaviors. And because special-needs children also often need extensive practice to retain a skill and generalize its use, a Home Activities Program, planned jointly by parents and teacher, can give them the necessary additional structured learning opportunities.

SEQUENTIAL CURRICULA: SUCCESS BY LEVELS

Each child and the teacher evaluate success. Success is built into the sequential curricula by levels of skills and teaching activities.

Each skill is divided into three levels: rudimentary Skill Level 1 and more refined Skill Levels 2 and 3. Each level is stated in observable behavioral movement terms. The skill levels become performance objectives. Children enter the sequential program at their own performance levels. As they add one small success to another and gain a new skill component or move to a higher skill level, they learn to listen, follow directions, practice, create, and play with others.

Within each skill level, your activities are sequenced, so the child can gain understanding progressively. Within each skill, you provide cues to meet each child's level of understanding and ability. The continuum of teaching cues is

1. verbal cues (action words) with physical assistance or prompts throughout the movement,

2. verbal cues and demonstrations,

3. verbal challenges and problem-solving cues such as "can you?" and

4. introduction of self-initiated learning activities.

GAMES

Game activities are identified for each performance objective by skill level in the seven activity books. At the end of each activity book is an alphabetized description of the games. This list includes the name of each game, formation, directions, equipment, skills involved in playing, and the type of play. Just before the list, you'll find selection criteria and ways to adapt games to different skill levels. Many of the game activities can be used to teach several objectives.

ACTION WORDS

Words for actions (step, look, catch, kick), objects (foot, ball, hand), and concepts (slow, fast, far) are used as verbal cues in teaching. These action words should be matched to the child's level of understanding. They provide a bridge to connect skill activities with other classroom learnings. In the seven activity books, action words are identified for each performance objective by skill level, and an alphabetized list of Action Words is provided at the beginning of each book. As you use this program, add words that are used in other classroom activities and delete those that the children are not ready to understand.

CHECKLISTS:
A CHILD'S RECORD OF PROGRESS

In each activity book, you'll also find Individual and Class Records of Progress listing each performance objective. You can use one or both to record the entry performance level and progress of each child. The child's Individual Record of Progress can be used as part of the Individualized Educational Program (IEP). The teacher can record the child's entry performance level and progress on the child's IEP report form or use the end-of-the-year checklist report.

By observing each child performing the skills in class (e.g., during play, during teaching of the skill or in set-aside time), you can meet the special needs of each child. By using the checklists to record each child's entry level performance of objectives to be taught, you can develop an instructional plan for and evaluate the progress of each child.

Assign each child a learning task (skill component or skill level) based on lesson objectives, and plan lesson activities based on the entry performance level to help the child achieve success. Then use the checklists to record, evaluate, and report each child's progress to the parents. With this record of progress, you can review the teaching-learning activities and can make changes to improve them as necessary.

TEACHING STRATEGY
Direct Instruction

Direct Instruction is coaching on specific tasks at a skill level that allows each child to succeed. A structured and sequential curriculum of essential skills is the primary component of Direct Instruction. As the child progresses in learning, the teacher poses verbal challenges and problem-solving questions such as "can you?" and "show me!" Direct Instruction is based on the premise that success builds success and failure breeds failure.

Adaptive Instruction

Adaptive Instruction is modifying what is taught and how it is taught in order to respond to each child's special needs. Adaptive Instruction helps teachers become more responsive to individual needs. Teaching is based on the child's abilities, on what is to be taught in the lesson, and on what the child is to achieve at the end of instruction. Lesson plans are based on the child's entry performance level on the skills to be taught. Students are monitored during instruction, and the activities are adjusted to each student's needs. Positive reinforcement is provided, and ways to correct the performance or behavior are immediately demonstrated.

Children enter the curriculum at different skill levels, and they learn at different rates. The sequential curriculum helps teachers to individualize the instruction for each child in the class. Thus, the same skill can be taught in a class that includes Betty, who enters at Skill Level 1, and James, who enters at Skill Level 3, because the activities are prescribed for the class or group, but the lesson is planned in order to focus on each child's learning task, and each child is working to achieve his or her own learning task. What is important is that each child master the essential skills at a level of performance that matches his or her abilities, interests, and joy.

Since children learn skills at different rates, you might want to use the following time estimates to allot instructional time for a child to make meaningful progress toward the desired level of performance. One or two skill components can usually be mastered in the instructional time available.

120 minutes	180 minutes	240 minutes	360 minutes
▲	▲	▲	▲

Higher Functioning Faster Learner			Slower Functioning Slower Learner

Play Skills and Activities

INTRODUCTION

Goals for Each Child

1. To demonstrate the ability to perform play skills taught in the instructional program;

2. To use play skills in daily living activities in order to maximize healthy development and joy in movement; and

3. To gain greater feelings of self-worth and self-confidence and to gain greater ability in moving to learn and learning to move.

The development of play skills is essential for all children. Most children learn play skills through the normal activities of childhood by interacting with their siblings, their peers, and their environment. Children with special needs, however, often lack opportunities to play with peers and have difficulty in developing appropriate play behavior. Since they do not develop play skills incidentally or spontaneously, these children need to be taught play skills as early as possible.

Careful planning and teaching are essential ingredients for children with special needs to acquire the skills to play with toys and playground equipment. This book presents three levels of activities for each play skill in the following order:

1. Hang from a Bar

2. Push and Pull an Object

3. Ride a Tricycle or Bicycle

4. Swing on a Swing

5. Travel on a Scooterboard

6. Slide Down a Slide

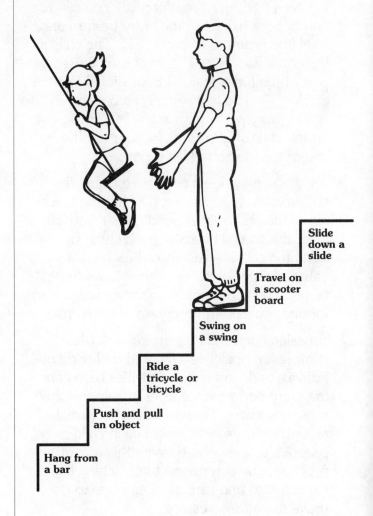

Slide down a slide

Travel on a scooter board

Swing on a swing

Ride a tricycle or bicycle

Push and pull an object

Hang from a bar

GETTING STARTED

To begin, decide which play skills you will teach. You can plan a unit or a week or a day or a year. You may decide to teach all skills in this book. Or you may select just a few. Review the checklist for each skill objective you select to teach. Become familiar with the skill components. Next, decide which action words and games you will use in teaching these skills.

Action Words

The words you use are teaching cues. Select ones your children will understand. For each of the play skills, action words are listed by skill level, and an alphabetized list of words for all the skills in this book is provided below. Circle the words you will use in teaching. If the words you selected prove too difficult for your students, cross them out. Add others that are more appropriate for your children. Star those words that work well.

ACTION	OBJECT	CONCEPT
Bend	Arm	Around
Bump	Back	Backward
Climb	Bar	Behind
Follow	Belly	Beside
Go	Bike	Between
Grasp	Block	Bottom
Grip	Box	Down
Hang	Feet	Forward
Hold	Floor	Hard
Kneel	Ground	High
Lean	Hand	Left
Lie	Handlebars	Look
Lift	Knee	Low
Lift up	Leg	Off
Move	Line	On
Place	Obstacle	Over
Point	Pedal	Ready
Pull	Pins	Right
Pump	Rails	Show me
Push	Rope	Sideways
Release	Scooterboard	Straight
Ride	Seat	Top
Sit	Side	Under
Slide	Slide	Up
Stand	Swing	
Step	Toy	
Stop	Wagon	
Swing		
Touch		
Turn		
Walk		

Games and Play Activities

In each skill level, you'll find a list of games; select the activity matched to the skills you plan to teach. At the end of this book, you'll find a list of games along with a description of each of them. You'll note that some of the games can be used to teach more than one skill. Use this master list to note those games and play activities that work well and those that do not. Make your comments right on the game listed, or set up a similar format for the games you have selected and make your comments on that sheet. This kind of information can help you plan successful teaching activities.

Equipment

One or more of the following pieces of equipment will be needed for most of the play activities and games:

1. Whistle for signals
2. Horizontal or parallel bars
3. Boxes or benches for sitting
4. Toy wagons, trucks, wheelbarrows, carts
5. Scooterboards
6. Tricycles or bicycles with training wheels
7. Traffic cones
8. Swings (chair, bucket, portable swing, tire)
9. Drum or record player
10. Balls
11. Ropes
12. Playground slide (3 to 10 feet)
13. Colored tape for paths
14. Landing mats

Space

Play skills require enough space for each child to move comfortably and safely. The size of the space depends on the equipment available for the activities and games selected and on the number of children in the class. A multipurpose room and a playground are desirable.

Health and Safety

Space and the equipment should be arranged for safety. Children with special visual needs may need a tour of the space and equipment before the lesson. A buddy can be assigned to be near the child when the lesson is taught. Children with special hearing needs may need to be close to the teacher or leader of the activity. The teacher should be positioned to observe all the children during the lesson activities. A very important rule is No standing on scooterboard, slide, or swing.

Organization: Learning Centers

Learning centers are one of the best types of class organization. You can plan small group learning centers when you know each child's level of performance of the play skill to be taught. Learning centers can be used to group children by levels of ability or to mix children of different levels of ability. The number of learning centers and their purpose will depend on the number of teachers and support personnel: aides, parent volunteers, older peer models.

To set up a learning center, you should consider the following:

1. **Purpose**	Skills to be taught and practiced
2. **Levels**	Levels 1, 2, and 3, or only one, determined by size of class, space, equipment, support personnel
3. **Grouping**	Same or mixed skill levels
4. **Physical setting**	Location, such as playground or multipurpose room; equipment available; existing physical boundaries, such as walls, or space to make boundaries with chairs, benches, mats, tapes
5. **Activities**	Type of game or instructional activity, such as running on paths, jumping over lines, climbing jungle gym

LEARNING CENTERS: PLAY SKILLS

LEARNING CENTER 1

Location: Multipurpose room, or playground

Skill: Push and pull objects

Activity: Rush down straight path, pull cart or wagon around cones, pull up incline

Grouping: Children at same or different skill levels

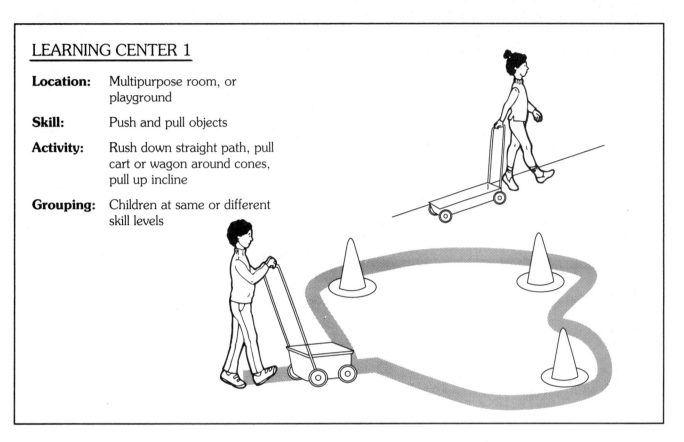

LEARNING CENTER 2

Location: Playground or multipurpose room

Skill: Ride a tricycle or bicycle

Activity: On straight path, on curved path, around obstacles

Grouping: Children at same or different skill levels

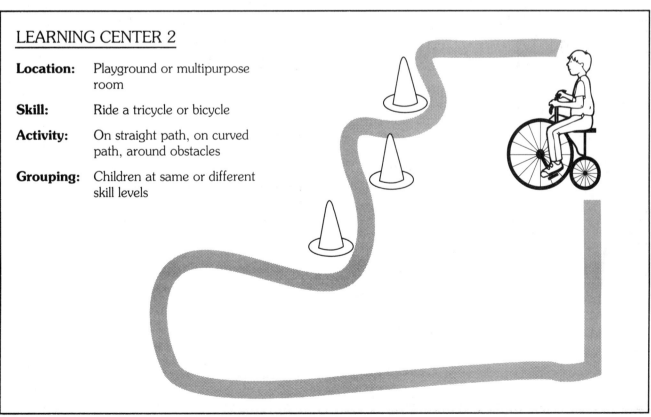

LEARNING CENTER 3

Location: Multipurpose room

Skill: Traveling on scooterboard

Activity: Travel under bar on "high-way" around obstacle

Grouping: Children at same or different skill levels

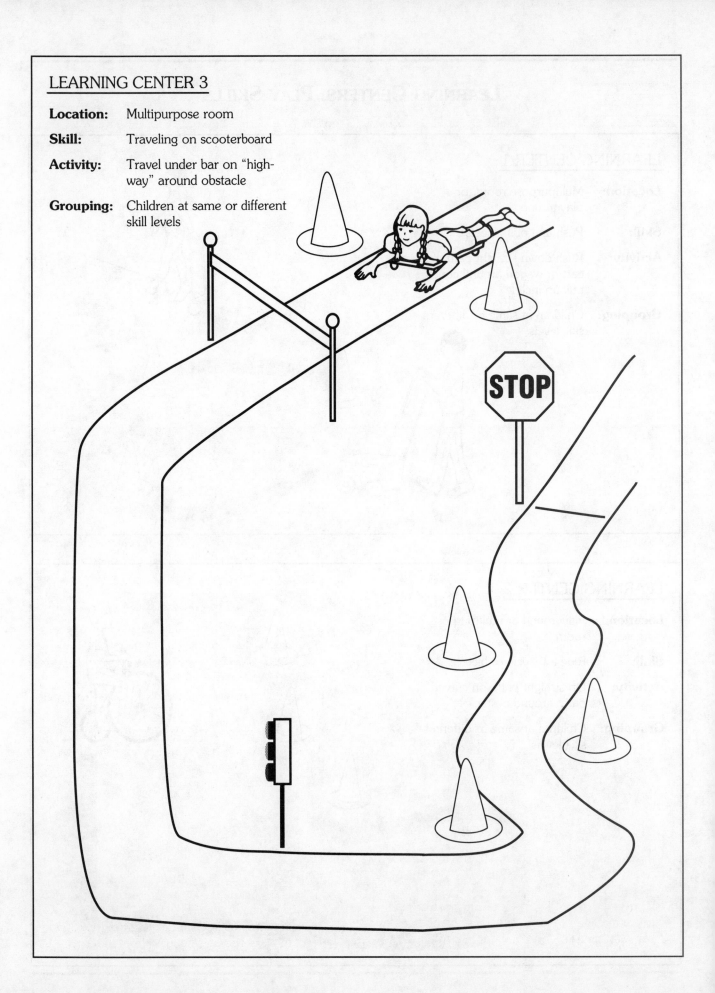

STOP

Play Activities

HANG FROM A BAR: SKILL LEVEL 1

Performance Objective

The child with ability to grasp and hold can hang from a bar with hands three consecutive times, demonstrating the following skill components:

The child can hang from a bar at shoulder height by

1. reaching up and grasping bar with hands, feet off ground, and hang for 5 seconds.

Action Words

Actions: Grasp, hang, hold, lift, place, release, stand, step, swing

Objects: Arm, bar, box, feet, hand, knee, leg

Concepts: Down, look, off, on, ready, show me, up

Games

- Did You Ever See a Lassie/Laddie?
- Do This, Do That
- Follow the Leader
- Monkey-Bar Hang Relay
- Obstacle Course
- Simon Says

TEACHING ACTIVITIES

If a child requires assistance to respond,

1. give verbal cues and physical assistance.
Manipulate or place child's hands on bar, and support the child's weight as he or she hangs from bar. Give the child specific verbal instructions throughout (in sign language, bliss symbols, action cues), such as "Hang from the bar," "Hold tightly," "Ready, hang."

2. give verbal cues with demonstration.
Use a model or have the child watch you hang from bar with hands in overhand grip. Then have the child perform the action. Use specific verbal instructions (as in 1 above with the modeling).

If a child can respond without assistance,

3. give a verbal challenge in the form of a problem: "Who can . . . ?" "Show me how you can . . ."
a. Hang from the bar and fall into a crash pad.
b. Swing back and forth while hanging from a bar.
c. Step off a bench or box while hanging from a bar, and swing back and forth three times and return feet to bench or box.
d. Jump up and grasp a bar 1"–4" above head and hang from it.
e. Variation: Hang to drumbeat until it stops.

4. introduce self-initiated learning activities.
Set up the mats and space for hanging from a bar. Provide time at the beginning of the lesson and free time for independent learning after the child understands the skills to be used. You may ask the child to create a game activity to play alone or with others (partner or small group) on the carpet squares or mats.

5. Variations: Set up an obstacle course that includes colored tape and mats, for hanging from a bar. Play a game, such as Did You Ever See a Lassie/Laddie? Follow the Leader or Do This, Do That, that incorporates hanging from the bar.

Performance Objective

The child with acquisition of Skill Level 1 and ability to bend knees and hold can hang from a bar by knees three consecutive times, demonstrating the following skill components:

The child can hang from a bar at shoulder height

2. with hands and knees for 5 seconds and then

3. release hands and hang with knees for 5 seconds.

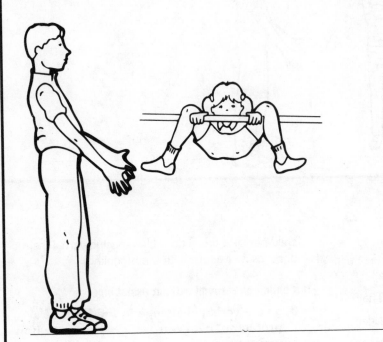

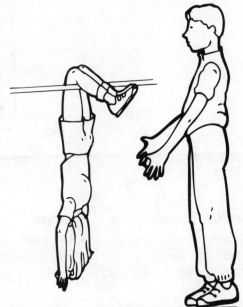

Skills to Review

1. Reach up and grasp bar with hands, feet off ground, and hang for 5 seconds.

Action Words

Actions: Grasp, hang, hold, lift, place, release, stand, step, swing

Objects: Arm, bar, box, feet, hand, knee, leg

Concepts: Down, look, off, on, ready, show me, up

Games

● Did You Ever See a Lassie/Laddie?

● Do This, Do That

● Follow the Leader

● Monkey-Bar Hang Relay

● Obstacle Course

● Simon Says

TEACHING ACTIVITIES

If a child requires assistance to respond,

1. give verbal cues and physical assistance.
Assist child in bringing one leg up to bar so that the child can hang from hands and knees. Have the child release hands from bar, then bring other leg up to the bar. Give the child specific verbal instructions throughout (in sign language, bliss symbols, action cues), such as "Hang from the bar with your knees and hands." "Hold tightly," "Ready, hang."

2. give verbal cues with demonstration.
Use a model or have the child watch you hang from bar with hands in overhand grip. Then have the child perform the action. Use specific verbal instructions (as in 1 above with the modeling).

If a child can respond without assistance,

3. **give a verbal challenge in the form of a problem: "Who can . . . ?" "Show me how you can . . ."**

a. Swing back and forth from bar by swinging arms.

b. Grab one bar with hands, using parallel bar, and swing legs to other bar, then release hands and hang from knees.

c. Swing from low bar, then increase height of bar.

d. Variations: Swing to beat of drum.

4. **introduce self-initiated learning activities.**
Set up the mats and space for hanging from a bar. Provide time at the beginning of the lesson and free time for independent learning after the child understands the skills to be used. You may ask the child to create a game activity to play alone or with others (partner or small group) on the carpet squares or mats.

5. **Variations:** Set up an obstacle course that includes colored tape and mats for hanging from a bar. Play a game, such as Did You Ever See a Lassie/Laddie? Follow the Leader, Do This, Do That, that incorporates hanging from the bar.

HANG FROM A BAR: SKILL LEVEL 3

Performance Objective

The child with acquisition of Skill Level 2 or a level of performance appropriate for the child's level of functioning can maintain that level over six weeks.

Given opportunity to use the skill, the child can
1. play two or more games listed below at home or school, and
2. play with equipment selected by teacher and parent(s).

Skills to Review

1. Level 1 bar hanging. Reach up and grasp bar with hands, feet off ground, and hang for 5 seconds.
2. Level 2 bar hanging. With hands and knees, hang for 5 seconds and then
3. release hands and hang with knees for 5 seconds.

Action Words

Actions: Grasp, hang, hold, lift, place, release, stand, step, swing

Objects: Arm, bar, box, feet, hand, knee, leg

Concepts: Down, look, off, on, ready, show me, up

Games

- Did You Ever See a Lassie/Laddie?
- Do This, Do That
- Follow the Leader
- Monkey-Bar Hang Relay
- Simon Says

TEACHING ACTIVITIES FOR MAINTENANCE

In Teaching

1. Provide the child with teaching cues (verbal and nonverbal, such as demonstration, modeling, imitating) for hanging from a bar that involve the skill components the child has achieved in compatible teaching and play activities. Bring to the child's attention the skill components he or she has already achieved. Provide positive reinforcement and feedback for the child.

2. Use games that require hanging from a bar and that involve imitating, modeling, and demonstrating.

3. Observe and assess each child's maintenance at the end of two weeks. Repeat at the end of four weeks (if maintained) and six weeks after initial date of attainment.

▲ Box in the skill level to be maintained on the child's Class Record of Progress. Note the date the child attained target level of performance (defined by teacher alone or co-planned with parents).

▲ Two weeks after attainment, observe the child. Is the level maintained? If child does not demonstrate the skill components at the desired level of performance, indicate the skill components that need reteaching or reinforcing in the comments sheet on the Class Record of Progress. Reschedule teaching time, and co-plan with parents the home activities necessary to reinforce child's achievement of the skill components and maintenance of attainment.

▲ Continue to observe the child, and reteach and reinforce until the child maintains that level of performance for six weeks.

▲ Plan teaching activities incorporating these components so that the child can continually use and reinforce them and can acquire new ones over the year.

▲ When the child can understand it, make a checklist poster illustrating the child's achievements. Bring the child's attention to these skill components in various compatible play and game activities throughout the year. Have the child help others—a partner or a small group.

In Co-Planning with Parent(s)

1. Encourage the parent(s) to reinforce the child's achievement of the skill components in everyday play and living activities in the home.

▲ Provide key action words for the parent(s) to emphasize.

▲ Give the parent(s) a list of play and games to use in playing with the child, thus reinforcing the skill components the child has achieved and needs support to maintain.

▲ Give the parent(s) a list of activities that can be done at home with the child, such as
   a. Hanging from suspended ladder by hands and knees.
   b. Hanging from jungle gym on the backyard bar with hands and knees.
   c. Hanging from bar for one minute, two minutes, etc.
   d. Hanging from a tree limb in backyard.

2. Set up a time every two weeks to interact with the parent(s) and exchange feedback on the child's progress.

PUSH AND PULL AN OBJECT: SKILL LEVEL 1

Performance Objective

The child with ability to grasp with hands and move can push an object (wagon, toy, scooter, box) with two hands three consecutive times, demonstrating the following skill components:

Within a clear space of 20 feet, the child can,

1. while moving forward, push an object with two hands for 10 feet and,
2. while moving forward, push an object with two hands around three obstacles 5 feet apart without bumping obstacles.

Action Words

Actions: Bump, grasp, hold, move, pull, push, step, walk

Objects: Arm, block, box, hand, obstacle, rope, scooterboard, toy, wagon

Concepts: Around, backward, forward, hard, sideways

Games

- Balloon Push
- Cageball Push
- Did You Ever See a Lassie/Laddie?
- Do This, Do That
- Follow the Leader
- Modified Shuffleboard
- Pushbroom
- Pushing a Box as a Group
- Sandbox Relay
- Simon Says
- Tug of War

TEACHING ACTIVITIES

If a child requires assistance to respond,

1. give verbal cues and physical assistance.
Manipulate child to push objects away from body by sitting or standing in back of child. Give the child specific verbal instructions throughout (in sign language, bliss symbols, action cues), such as "Push the truck," "Turn hard."

2. give verbal cues with demonstration.
Use a model or have the child watch you push an object away. Then have the child perform the action. Use specific verbal instructions (as in 1 above with the modeling).

If a child can respond without assistance,

3. give a verbal challenge in the form of a problem: "Who can . . . ?" "Show me how you can . . ."
a. Push the car or ball away.
b. Push the tower of blocks so that they fall down.
c. Push the box (with tires in it) to me.
d. Push the cookie cutter into the clay.
e. Push the wheelbarrow filled with sand.
f. Variations: Push objects on various surfaces (cement, sand, grass). Push only to music.

4. introduce self-initiated learning activities.
Set up the equipment and space for pushing and pulling. Provide time at the beginning of the lesson and free time for independent learning after the child understands the skills to be used. You may ask the child to create a game activity to play alone or with others (partner or small group), using the equipment.

5. Variations: Set up an obstacle course that includes colored tape and mats, to perform pushing and pulling. Play a game, such as Pushbroom, Tug of War, or Simon Says, that incorporates pushing and pulling objects.

PUSH AND PULL AN OBJECT: SKILL LEVEL 2

Performance Objective

The child with acquisition of Skill Level 1 can pull an object (wagon, toy, scooter, box) three consecutive times, demonstrating the following skill components:

Within a clear space of 20 feet, the child can,

3. while moving backward, pull an object with one or two hands for 10 feet and,

4. while moving forward, pull an object with one or two hands for 10 feet and

5. pull an object with one or two hands around three obstacles aligned 5 feet apart without bumping obstacles.

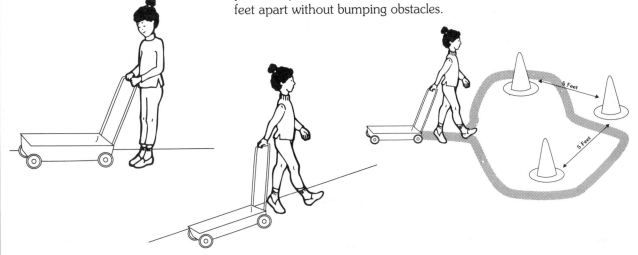

Skills to Review

1. While moving forward, push an object with two hands for 10 feet and,

2. while moving forward, push an object with two hands around three obstacles 5 feet apart without bumping obstacles.

Action Words

Actions: Bump, grasp, hold, move, pull, push, step, walk

Objects: Arm, block, box, hand, obstacle, rope, scooterboard, toy, wagon

Concepts: Around, backward, forward, hard, sideways

Games

- Balloon Push
- Cageball Push
- Did You Ever See a Lassie/Laddie?
- Do This, Do That
- Follow the Leader
- Modified Shuffleboard
- Pushbroom
- Pushing a Box as a Group
- Sandbox Relay
- Simon Says
- Tug of War

TEACHING ACTIVITIES

If a child requires assistance to respond,

1. give verbal cues and physical assistance.
Manipulate and stand behind child, and hold his or her hands on wagon handle. Walk backward and pull the wagon. Then have the child walk forward, and assist the child to pull wagon from his or her rear. Give the child specific verbal instructions throughout (in sign language, bliss symbols, action cues), such as "Go get the wagon," "Hold on to it with your hand," "Pull it here."

2. give verbal cues with demonstration.
Use a model or have the child watch you pull the wagon around the obstacles. Have the child pull a toy and follow you around the obstacles. Then have the child pull the toy around obstacles alone. Use specific verbal instructions (as in 1 above with the modeling).

If a child can respond without assistance,

3. give a verbal challenge in the form of a problem: "Who can . . . ?" "Show me how you can . . ."
a. Pull a toy or wagon across the room.
b. Pull a child on the wagon. Have the child pull you.

c. Pull wagon around obstacles and through large cardboard boxes.

d. Pull a wagon along the colored tape (highway).

e. Variations: Pull an object to music. Pull an object over various terrains (grass, sand, cement, dirt).

4. introduce self-initiated learning activities. Set up the equipment and space for pushing and pulling. Provide time at the beginning of the lesson and free time for independent learning after the child understands the skills to be used. You may ask the child to create a game activity to play alone or with others (partner or small group), using the equipment.

5. Variations: Set up an obstacle course that includes colored tape and mats to perform pushing and pulling. Play a game, such as Pushbroom, Tug of War, or Simon Says, that incorporates pushing and pulling objects.

PUSH AND PULL AN OBJECT: SKILL LEVEL 3

Performance Objective

The child with acquisition of Skill Level 2 or a level of performance appropriate for the child's level of functioning can maintain that level over six weeks.

Given opportunity to use the skill, the child can

1. play two or more games listed below at home or school, and
2. play with equipment selected by teacher and parent(s).

Skills to Review

1. Level 1 pushing and pulling. While moving forward, push an object with two hands for 10 feet and,
2. while moving forward, push an object with two hands around three obstacles 5 feet apart without bumping obstacles.
3. Level 2 pushing and pulling. While moving backward, pull an object with one or two hands for 10 feet and,
4. while moving forward, pull an object with one or two hands for 10 feet and
5. pull an object with one or two hands around three obstacles 5 feet apart without bumping obstacles.

Action Words

Actions: Bump, grasp, hold, move, pull, push, step, walk

Objects: Arm, block, box, hand, obstacle, rope, scooterboard, toy, wagon

Concepts: Around, backward, forward, hard, sideways

Games

- Balloon Push
- Cageball Push
- Did You Ever See a Lassie/Laddie?
- Do This, Do That
- Follow the Leader
- Modified Shuffleboard
- Pushbroom
- Pushing a Box as a Group
- Sandbox Relay
- Simon Says
- Tug of War

TEACHING ACTIVITIES FOR MAINTENANCE

In Teaching

1. Provide the child with teaching cues (verbal and nonverbal, such as demonstration, modeling, imitating) for pushing and pulling objects that involve the skill components the child has achieved in compatible teaching and play activities. Bring to the child's attention the skill components he or she has already achieved. Provide positive reinforcement and feedback for the child.
2. Use games that require pushing and pulling objects and that involve imitating, modeling, and demonstrating.
3. Observe and assess each child's maintenance at the end of two weeks. Repeat at the end of four weeks (if maintained) and six weeks after initial date of attainment.

▲ Box in the skill level to be maintained on the child's Class Record of Progress. Note the date the child attained target level of performance (defined by teacher alone or co-planned with parents).

▲ Two weeks after attainment, observe the child. Is the level maintained? If child does not demonstrate the skill components at the desired level of performance, indicate the skill components that need reteaching or reinforcing in the comments sheet on the Class Record of Progress. Reschedule teaching time, and co-plan with parents the home activities to reinforce child's achievement of the skill components and maintenance of attainment.

▲ Continue to observe the child, and reteach and reinforce until the child maintains that level of performance for six weeks.

▲ Plan teaching activities incorporating these components so that the child can continually use and reinforce them and can acquire new ones over the year.

▲ When the child can understand it, make a checklist poster illustrating the child's achievements. Bring the child's attention to these skill components in various compatible play and game activities throughout the year. Have the child help others—a partner or a small group.

In Co-Planning with Parent(s)

1. Encourage the parent(s) to reinforce the child's achievement of the skill components in everyday play and living activities in the home.

▲ Provide key action words for the parent(s) to emphasize.

▲ Give the parent(s) a list of play and games to use in playing with the child, thus reinforcing the skill components the child has achieved and needs support to maintain.

▲ Give the parent(s) a list of activities that can be done at home with the child, such as
   a. Pulling or pushing wagon up the ramp.
   b. Pulling or pushing wagon over there.
   c. Pushing or pulling another child around in raft.
   d. Pulling or pushing wagon around cones in obstacle course.
   e. Pushing or pulling a friend across room on a scooterboard.
   f. Climbing cargo net, pulling with your arms; then move your legs.
   g. Pulling on the tug-of-war rope across the center line.
   h. Pulling on a rope to make a bell ring.
   i. Variations: Pulling or pushing on various surfaces (grass, sand, sidewalk, dirt).

2. Set up a time every two weeks to interact with the parent(s) and exchange feedback on the child's progress.

RIDE A TRICYCLE OR BICYCLE: SKILL LEVEL 1

Performance Objective

The child with ability to sit, grasp bars, and move legs or to bicycle with training wheels three consecutive times, demonstrating the following skill components:

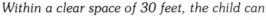

Within a clear space of 30 feet, the child can

1. assume ready position by sitting on tricycle or bicycle and grasping handlebars, with feet maintaining contact on pedals, and be pushed 10 feet or more and then

2. assume ready position by sitting on tricycle or bicycle and grasping handlebars, with feet maintaining contact on pedals, and push down with right foot on up pedal and push down with left foot on up pedal, riding 10 feet or more.

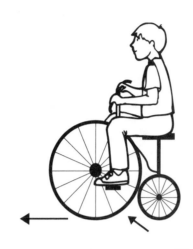
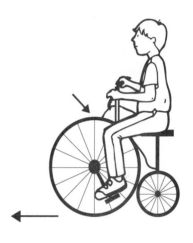

Action Words

Actions: Follow, go, hold, lift up, push, ride, sit, turn

Objects: Bike, feet, hand, handlebars, knee, line, pedal, seat

Concepts: Around, behind, down, forward, left, look, on, over, ready, right, show me, under, up

Games

- Base Running
- Bike Relay
- Crossing the Lake
- Did You Ever See a Lassie/Laddie?
- Do This, Do That
- Follow the Leader
- Freeze
- Giants and Dragons
- Hill Dill
- Hot Rods
- Jet Pilots
- Obstacle Course
- Simon Says

TEACHING ACTIVITIES

If a child requires assistance to respond,

1. give verbal cues and physical assistance.
Manipulate and assist child by alternately pushing down on the child's knees or feet so that he or she can pedal the tricycle or bicycle. Use velcro straps on feet and hands if necessary. Use different colored tape on each pedal to cue child to step down. Give the child specific verbal instructions throughout (in sign language, bliss symbols, action cues), such as "Sit on the bike," "Push the pedals," "Ride to me."

2. give verbal cues with demonstration.
Use a model or have the child watch you ride bike, alternately pushing down on pedals. Have child ride bike after you. Use specific verbal instructions (as in 1 above with the modeling).

If a child can respond without assistance,

3. give a verbal challenge in the form of a problem: "Who can . . . ?" "Show me how you can . . ."

a. Ride the tricycle (bike) down the incline to me.
b. Ride the tricycle (bike) along the taped straight line on the floor.
c. Ride across the play area to me.
d. Variations: Ride on different surfaces (room, gym, cement, carpet). Ride to music, stop when music stops.

4. introduce self-initiated learning activities.
Set up the equipment (mats) and space for riding tricycle or bicycle. Provide time at the beginning of the lesson and free time for independent learning after the child understands the skills to be used. You may ask the child to create a game activity to play alone or with others (partner or small group), using equipment.

5. Variations: Set up an obstacle course that includes colored tape and mats to ride a tricycle or bicycle. Play a game, such as Base Riding, Crossing the Lake, or Hot Rods, that incorporates riding tricycle or bicycle.

RIDE A TRICYCLE OR BICYCLE: SKILL LEVEL 2

Performance Objective

The child with acquisition of Skill Level 1 can ride a tricycle or bicycle with training wheels three consecutive times, demonstrating the following skill components:

Within a clear space of 30 feet, the child can

3. assume ready position by sitting on bike and grasping handlebars, with feet on pedals in up position, and push down with right foot, then push down with left foot, riding a distance of 20 feet or more and

4. assume ready position by sitting on bike and grasping handlebars, with feet on pedals, and ride the bike around three obstacles aligned 10 feet apart without bumping obstacles.

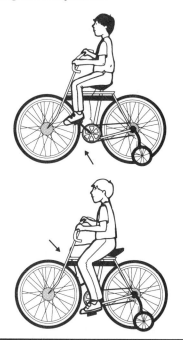

10 Feet

10 Feet

Skills to Review

1. Assume ready position by sitting on bike and grasping handlebars, with feet maintaining contact with pedals, and be pushed 10 feet or more and then

2. assume ready position by sitting on bike and grasping handlebars, with feet maintaining contact with pedals, and push down with right foot on up pedal and push down with left foot on up pedal, riding 10 feet or more.

Action Words

Actions: Follow, go, hold, lift up, push, ride, sit, turn

Objects: Bike, feet, hand, handlebars, knee, line, pedal, seat

Concepts: Around, behind, down, forward, left, look, on, over, ready, right, show me, under, up

Games

- Base Running
- Bike Relay
- Crossing the Lake
- Did You Ever See a Lassie/Laddie?
- Do This, Do That
- Follow the Leader
- Freeze
- Giants and Dragons
- Hill Dill
- Hot Rods
- Jet Pilots
- Obstacle Course
- Simon Says

TEACHING ACTIVITIES

If a child requires assistance to respond,

1. **give verbal cues and physical assistance.**
Tap the child's knee when pedal is in the up position to cue child to push down. Have the child pull on red or blue side to turn bike. Give the child specific verbal instructions throughout (in sign language, bliss symbols, action cues), such as "Sit on the bike," "Push the pedals," "Ride to me."

2. **give verbal cues with demonstration.**
Use a model or have the child watch you ride a bike. Have child ride a tricycle, following another child around the obstacles. Use specific verbal instructions (as in 1 above with the modeling).

If a child can respond without assistance,

3. **give a verbal challenge in the form of a problem: "Who can . . . ?" "Show me how you can . . ."**
   a. Ride your bike on the taped line on the floor.
   b. Follow another child around on your bike; then you become the leader.
   c. Ride around the cones; pull on the red or blue side to turn the tricycle.
   d. Ride your bike (along with other children) as fast as you can to me. Who will be the fastest?
   e. Variations: Ride on different surfaces (room, gym, cement, carpet). Ride to music.

4. **introduce self-initiated learning activities.**
Set up the equipment (mats) and space for riding tricycle or bicycle. Provide time at the beginning of the lesson and free time for independent learning after the child understands the skills to be used. You may ask the child to create a game activity to play alone or with others (partner or small group), using the equipment.

5. **Variations:** Set up an obstacle course that includes colored tape, mats to ride through on a tricycle or bicycle. Play a game, such as Base Riding, Crossing the Lake, or Hot Rods, that incorporates riding tricycle or bicycle.

RIDE A TRICYCLE OR BICYCLE: SKILL LEVEL 3

Performance Objective

The child with acquisition of Skill Level 2 or a level of performance appropriate for the child's level of functioning can maintain that level over six weeks.

Given opportunity to use the skill, the child can

1. play two or more games listed below at home or school, and
2. play with equipment selected by teacher and parent(s).

Skills to Review

1. Level 1 riding. Assume ready position by sitting on bike and grasping handlebars, with feet maintaining contact on pedals, and be pushed 10 feet or more and

2. assume ready position by sitting on bike and grasping handlebars, with feet maintaining contact on pedals, and push down with right foot on up pedal, push down with left foot on up pedal, riding 10 feet or more.

3. Level 2. Assume ready position by sitting on bike and grasping handlebars, with feet on pedals in up position, and push down with right foot, then push down with left foot, riding a distance of 20 feet or more and

4. assume ready position by sitting on bike and grasping handlebars, with feet on pedals, and ride the bike around three obstacles aligned 10 feet apart without bumping obstacles.

Action Words

Actions: Follow, go, hold, lift up, push, ride, sit, turn

Objects: Bike, feet, hand, handlebars, knee, line, pedal, seat

Concepts: Around, behind, down, forward, left, look, on, over, ready, right, show me, under, up

Games

- Base Running
- Bike Relay
- Crossing the Lake
- Did You Ever See a Lassie/Laddie?
- Do This, Do That
- Follow the Leader
- Freeze
- Giants and Dragons
- Hill Dill
- Hot Rods
- Jet Pilots
- Obstacle Course
- Simon Says

TEACHING ACTIVITIES FOR MAINTENANCE

In Teaching

1. Provide the child with teaching cues (verbal and nonverbal, such as demonstration, modeling, imitating) for riding a tricycle or bicycle that involve the skill components the child has achieved in compatible teaching and play activities. Bring to the child's attention the skill components he or she has already achieved. Provide positive reinforcement and feedback for the child.

2. Use games that require riding a tricycle or bicycle and that involve imitating, modeling, and demonstrating.

3. Observe and assess each child's maintenance at the end of two weeks. Repeat at the end of four weeks (if maintained) and six weeks after initial date of attainment.

▲ Box in the skill level to be maintained on the child's Class Record of Progress. Note the date the child attained target level of performance (defined by teacher alone or co-planned with parents).

▲ Two weeks after attainment, observe the child. Is the level maintained? If child does not demonstrate the skill components at the desired level of performance, indicate the skill components that need reteaching or reinforcing in the comments sheet on the Class Record of Progress. Reschedule teaching time, and co-plan with parents the home activities necessary to reinforce child's achievement of the skill components and maintenance of attainment.

▲ Continue to observe the child, and reteach and reinforce until the child maintains that level of performance for six weeks.

▲ Plan teaching activities incorporating these components so that the child can continually use and reinforce them and can acquire new ones over the year.

▲ When the child can understand it, make a checklist poster illustrating the child's achievements. Bring the child's attention to these skill components in various compatible play and game activities throughout the year. Have the child help others—a partner or a small group.

In Co-Planning with Parent(s)

1. Encourage the parent(s) to reinforce the child's achievement of the skill components in everyday play and living activities in the home.

▲ Provide key action words for the parent(s) to emphasize.

▲ Give the parent(s) a list of play and games to use in playing with the child, thus reinforcing the skill components the child has achieved and needs support to maintain.

▲ Give the parent(s) a list of activities that can be done at home with the child, such as
   a. Riding around different objects (chairs, boxes, cones) on a tricycle or bicycle.
   b. Riding around the large figure 8 course (racing track). Go both ways.
   c. Riding your bike around the neighborhood block.
   d. Riding your bike around the park playground.
   e. Riding your bike up and down hills.
   f. Variations: Riding on different surfaces (room, gym, cement, carpet). Riding to music.

2. Set up a time every two weeks to interact with the parent(s) and exchange feedback on the child's progress.

Performance Objective

The child with ability to grasp and sit on a swing can swing three consecutive times, demonstrating the following skill components:

On a swing adjusted so that the child's feet touch the ground, the child can

1. sit and be pushed in 4- to 6-foot arc for five or more pushes and then,

2. pushing with feet against ground, initiate swinging in a 2- to 4-foot arc for three cycles (forward and backward).

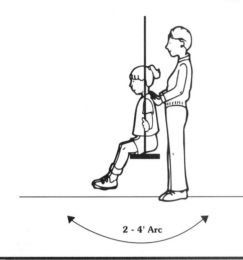

2 - 4' Arc

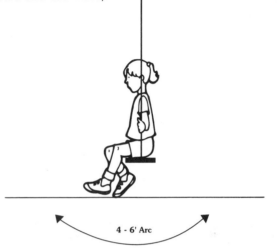

4 - 6' Arc

Action Words

Actions: Bend, lean, pump, push, sit, swing

Objects: Arm, feet, ground, hand, seat, swing

Concepts: Backward, down, forward, hard, high, look, low, on, up

Games

- Did You Ever See a Lassie/Laddie?
- Do This, Do That
- Follow the Leader
- How High Can You Fly?
- Obstacle Course
- Simon Says

TEACHING ACTIVITIES

If a child requires assistance to respond,

1. give verbal cues and physical assistance.
Manipulate and assist child to swing by standing behind child, and raise or lower height of seat so that child's feet touch ground. Have child push against ground to imitate swing. Give the child specific verbal instructions throughout (in sign language, bliss symbols, action cues), such as "Sit on the swing," "Push with your feet," "Ready, swing."

2. give verbal cues with demonstration.
Use a model or have the child watch you initiate swinging by pushing with feet against ground. Then have the child perform the action. Use specific verbal instructions (as in 1 above with the modeling).

If a child can respond without assistance,

3. give a verbal challenge in the form of a problem: "Who can . . . ?" "Show me how you can . . ."
a. On the swing, push off the ground with your feet.
b. Swing on the bucket swing.
c. Variations: Use different swings (bucket, belt, chair, tire, doorway swing). Use footprints on ground for foot placement while pushing.

4. introduce self-initiated learning activities.
Set up the equipment and space for swinging on a swing. Provide time at the beginning of the lesson and free time for independent learning after the child understands the skills to be used. You may ask the child to create a game activity to play alone or with others (partner or small group), using the equipment.

5. Variations: Set up an obstacle course that includes colored tape to swing on a swing. Play a game, such as How High Can You Fly? or Follow the Leader, that incorporates swinging on a swing.

SWING ON A SWING: SKILL LEVEL 2

Performance Objective

The child with acquisition of Skill Level 1 can initiate swinging and pumping on a swing three consecutive times, demonstrating the following skill components:

On a swing adjusted so that the child's feet touch the ground, the child can

3. lean back, extending legs, as swing moves forward, and lean forward, bending knees, as swing moves backward in a 2- to 4-foot arc for five cycles and then

4. swing forward and backward in a 4- to 6-foot arc for ten cycles.

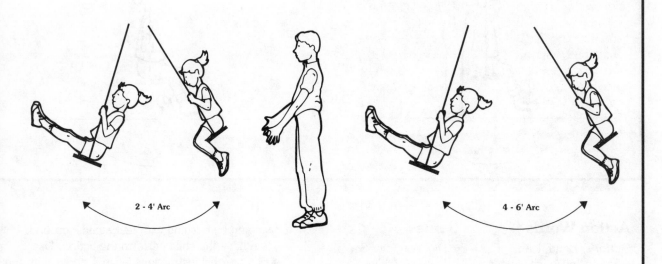

2 - 4' Arc

4 - 6' Arc

Skills to Review

1. Sit and be pushed in 4- to 6-foot arc for five or more pushes and then,

2. pushing with feet against ground, initiate swinging in 2- to 4-foot arc for three cycles (forward and backward).

Action Words

Actions: Bend, lean, pump, push, sit, swing

Objects: Arm, feet, ground, hand, seat, swing

Concepts: Backward, down, forward, hard, high, look, low, on, up

Games

• Did You Ever See a Lassie/Laddie?

• Do This, Do That

• Follow the Leader

• How High Can You Fly?

• Obstacle Course

• Simon Says

TEACHING ACTIVITIES

If a child requires assistance to respond,

1. give verbal cues and physical assistance.
Have child sit in your lap as you swing. Have child pump back and forth by extending legs and leaning back and bending knees and leaning forward. Give the child specific verbal instructions throughout (in sign language, bliss symbols, action cues), such as "Sit in the swing," "Pump your legs back and forth," "Ready, swing."

2. give verbal cues with demonstration.
Use a model or have the child watch you initiate swinging by pushing with feet against the ground. Then have the child perform the action. Use specific verbal instructions (as in 1 above with the modeling).

If a child can respond without assistance,

3. **give a verbal challenge in the form of a problem: "Who can . . . ?" "Show me how you can . . ."**
   a. Pump on the swing and touch my hand (teacher stands in front of swing).
   b. Pump on the swing three times back and forth.
   c. How high can you pump the swing?
   d. Variations: Use different swings (bucket belt, chair, tire, doorway swing). Use footprints on ground for foot placement while pushing.

4. **introduce self-initiated learning activities.**
Set up the equipment and space for swinging on a swing. Provide time at the beginning of the lesson and free time for independent learning after the child understands the skills to be used. You may ask the child to create a game activity to play alone or with others (partner or small group), using the equipment.

5. **Variations:** Set up an obstacle course that includes colored tape to swing on a swing. Play a game, such as How High Can You Fly? or Follow the Leader, that incorporates swinging on a swing.

SWING ON A SWING: SKILL LEVEL 3

Performance Objective

The child with acquisition of Skill Level 2 or a level of performance appropriate for the child's level of functioning can maintain that level over six weeks.

Given opportunity to use the skill, the child can

1. play two or more games listed below at home or school, and
2. play with equipment selected by teacher and parent(s).

Skills to Review

1. Level 1 swinging. Sit and be pushed in 4- to 6-foot arc for five or more pushes and then,
2. pushing with feet against ground, initiate swinging in 2- to 4-foot arc for three cycles (forward and backward).
3. Level 2 swinging. Lean back, extending legs, as swing moves forward, and lean forward, bending knees, as swing moves backward in 2- to 4-foot arc for five cycles and then
4. swing forward and backward in 4- to 6-foot arc for ten cycles.

Action Words

Actions: Bend, lean, pump, push, sit, swing

Objects: Arm, feet, ground, hand, seat, swing

Concepts: Backward, down, forward, hard, high, look, low, on, up

Games

- Did You Ever See a Lassie/Laddie?
- Do This, Do That
- Follow the Leader
- How High Can You Fly?
- Obstacle Course
- Simon Says

TEACHING ACTIVITIES FOR MAINTENANCE

In Teaching

1. Provide the child with teaching cues (verbal and nonverbal, such as demonstration, modeling, imitating) for swinging on a swing that involve the skill components the child has achieved in compatible teaching and play activities. Bring to the child's attention the skill components he or she has already achieved. Provide positive reinforcement and feedback for the child.

2. Use games that require swinging on a swing and that involve imitating, modeling, and demonstrating.

3. Observe and assess each child's maintenance at the end of two weeks. Repeat at the end of four weeks (if maintained) and six weeks after initial date of attainment.

▲ Box in the skill level to be maintained on the child's Class Record of Progress. Note the date the child attained target level of performance (defined by teacher alone or co-planned with parents).

▲ Two weeks after attainment, observe the child. Is the level maintained? If child does not demonstrate the skill components at the desired level of performance, indicate the skill components that need reteaching or reinforcing in the comments sheet on the Class Record of Progress. Reschedule teaching time, and co-plan with parents the home activities necessary to reinforce child's achievement of the skill components and maintenance of attainment.

▲ Continue to observe the child, and reteach and reinforce until the child maintains that level of performance for six weeks.

▲ Plan teaching activities incorporating these components so that the child can continually use and reinforce them and can acquire new ones over the year.

▲ When the child can understand it, make a check-list poster illustrating the child's achievements. Bring the child's attention to these skill components in various compatible play and game activities throughout the year. Have the child help others—a partner or a small group.

In Co-Planning with Parent(s)

1. Encourage the parent(s) to reinforce the child's achievement of the skill components in everyday play and living activities in the home.

▲ Provide key action words for the parent(s) to emphasize.

▲ Give the parent(s) a list of play and games to use in playing with the child, thus reinforcing the skill components the child has achieved and needs support to maintain.

▲ Give the parent(s) a list of activities that can be done at home with the child, such as
   a. How long can you swing without my help?
   b. Swinging up high on the backyard swing set.
   c. Can you swing higher on the chair swing or bucket swing?
   d. Can you swing from a tire hung from the oak tree in your yard?
   e. Variations: Use different swings (bucket belt, chair, tire, doorway swing). Use footprints on ground for foot placement while pushing.

2. Set up a time every two weeks to interact with the parent(s) and exchange feedback on the child's progress.

TRAVEL ON A SCOOTERBOARD: SKILL LEVEL 1

Performance Objective

The child with ability to sit, kneel, or lie on a scooterboard and move arms and/or legs can travel on the scooterboard three consecutive times, demonstrating the following skill components:

Within a clear space of 30 feet, the child can

1. assume ready position on scooterboard and be pushed without falling off for 10 feet or more and then
2. assume ready position on scooterboard and push with hands or feet, traveling 5 feet or more in any direction.

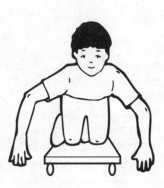

Action Words

Actions: Go, hold, kneel, lie, pull, push, ride, sit, turn

Objects: Back, belly, hand, knee, pins, scooterboard, seat

Concepts: Around, backward, beside, between, forward, look, ready, show me, sideways, straight

Games

- Base Running
- Circle Strike Ball
- Crossing the Lake
- Did You Ever See a Lassie/Laddie?
- Do This, Do That
- Follow the Leader
- Freeze
- Giants and Dragons
- Hill Dill
- Hot Rods
- Jet Pilots
- Obstacle Course
- Scooterboard Races
- Simon Says

TEACHING ACTIVITIES

If a child requires assistance to respond,

1. give verbal cues and physical assistance.
Manipulate or assist child to propel the scooterboard by walking alongside him or her. Place one hand on child's back and the other on scooterboard. Push child to assist in propelling scooterboard. Give the child specific verbal instructions throughout (in sign language, bliss symbols, action cues), such as "Move on the scooterboard," "Come to me now."

2. give verbal cues with demonstration.
Use a model or have the child watch you move on scooterboard. Then have the child perform the same action. Use specific verbal instructions (as in 1 above with the modeling).

If a child can respond without assistance,

3. give a verbal challenge in the form of a problem: "Who can . . . ?" "Show me how you can . . ."

a. Propel yourself on the scooterboard with hands and feet to me.

b. Propel yourself on the scooterboard under table.

c. Propel yourself on the scooterboard up and down incline.

d. Travel on the scooterboard to the ball, push it forward, and chase it.

e. Propel yourself on the scooterboard and travel to music.

f. Variations: Propel yourself on the scooterboard and travel on different surfaces (cement, carpet, blacktop).

4. introduce self-initiated learning activities.
Set up the equipment and space for using a scooterboard. Provide time at the beginning of the lesson and free time for independent learning after the child understands the skills to be used. You may ask the child to create a game activity to play alone or with others (partner or small group) on the equipment.

5. Variations: Set up an obstacle course that includes colored tape to travel on a scooterboard. Play a game, such as Base Running, Circle Strike Ball, or Hot Rods, that incorporates using a scooterboard.

TRAVEL ON A SCOOTERBOARD: SKILL LEVEL 2

Performance Objective

The child with acquisition of Skill Level 1 can assume a ready position traveling on a scooterboard three consecutive times, demonstrating the following skill components:

Within a clear space of 30 feet, the child can

3. travel on scooterboard in a 5-foot-wide path for 15 feet or more and

4. travel on scooterboard around three obstacles aligned 5 feet apart without bumping obstacles.

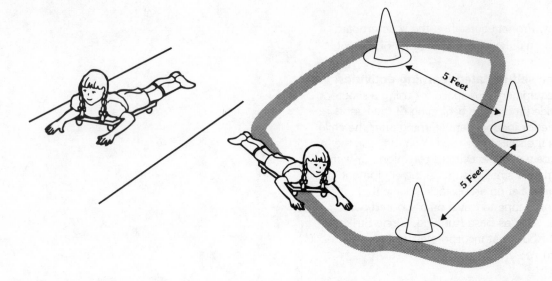

Skills to Review

1. Assume ready position on scooterboard and be pushed without falling off for 10 feet or more and then

2. assume ready position on scooterboard and push with hands or feet, traveling 5 feet or more in any direction.

Action Words

Actions: Go, hold, kneel, lie, pull, push, ride, sit, turn

Objects: Back, belly, hand, knee, pins, scooterboard, seat

Concepts: Around, backward, beside, between, forward, look, ready, show me, sideways, straight

Games

- Base Running
- Circle Strike Ball
- Crossing the Lake
- Did You Ever See a Lassie/Laddie?
- Do This, Do That
- Follow the Leader
- Freeze
- Giants and Dragons
- Hill Dill
- Hot Rods
- Jet Pilots
- Obstacle Course
- Scooterboard Races
- Simon Says

TEACHING ACTIVITIES

If a child requires assistance to respond,

1. give verbal cues and physical assistance.
Assist child to lie prone on scooterboard. Position child's feet against the wall, and have child push off hard and travel in a straight path. Give the child specific verbal instructions throughout (in sign language, bliss symbols, action cues), such as "Move on the scooterboard," "Go straight or around the cones," "Come to me."

2. give verbal cues with demonstration.
Use a model or have the child watch you travel on the scooterboard in a straight path and around obstacles by changing directions. Then have the child perform the action. Use specific verbal instructions (as in 1 above with the modeling).

If a child can respond without assistance,

3. give a verbal challenge in the form of a problem: "Who can . . . ?" "Show me how you can . . ."

a. Travel on the scooterboard down the center of the marked path (5' x 5').

b. Travel on scooterboard in a straight path under the table and through the box.

c. Race with your friend in a straight path on the scooterboard.

d. Try to knock down the pins or milk cartons as you pass them on the scooterboard.

e. Travel on the scooterboard around the obstacles.

f. Travel around the circle around the cones on the scooterboard.

g. Variations: Move to music. Move on different surfaces (cement, carpet, blacktop).

4. introduce self-initiated learning activities.
Set up the equipment and space for using a scooterboard. Provide time at the beginning of the lesson and free time for independent learning after the child understands the skills to be used. You may ask the child to create a game activity to play alone or with others (partner or small group) on the equipment.

5. Variations: Set up an obstacle course that includes colored tape to ride on a scooterboard. Play a game, such as Base Running, Circle Strike Ball, or Hot Rods, that incorporates using a scooterboard.

TRAVEL ON A SCOOTERBOARD: SKILL LEVEL 3

Performance Objective

The child with acquisition of Skill Level 2 or a level of performance appropriate for the child's level of functioning can maintain that level over six weeks.

Given opportunity to use the skill, the child can

1. play two or more games listed below at home or school, and
2. play with equipment selected by teacher and parent(s).

Skills to Review

1. Level 1 scooterboard traveling. Assume ready position on scooterboard and be pushed without falling off for 10 feet or more and then
2. assume ready position on a scooterboard and push with hands or feet, traveling 5 feet or more in any direction.
3. Level 2 scooterboard traveling. Travel on scooterboard in a 5-foot-wide path for 15 or more feet and
4. travel on scooterboard around three obstacles aligned 5 feet apart without bumping obstacles.

Action Words

Actions: Go, hold, kneel, lie, pull, push, ride, sit, turn

Objects: Back, belly, hand, knee, pins, scooterboard, seat

Concepts: Around, backward, beside, between, forward, look, ready, show me, sideways, straight

Games

- Base Running
- Circle Strike Ball
- Crossing the Lake
- Did You Ever See a Lassie/Laddie?
- Do This, Do That
- Follow the Leader
- Freeze
- Giants and Dragons
- Hill Dill
- Hot Rods
- Jet Pilots
- Obstacle Course
- Scooterboard Races
- Simon Says

TEACHING ACTIVITIES FOR MAINTENANCE

In Teaching

1. Provide the child with teaching cues (verbal and nonverbal, such as demonstration, modeling, imitating) for using a scooterboard that involve the skill components the child has achieved in compatible teaching and play activities. Bring to the child's attention the skill components he or she has already achieved. Provide positive reinforcement and feedback for the child.
2. Use games that require using scooterboard and that involve imitating, modeling, and demonstrating.
3. Observe and assess each child's maintenance at the end of two weeks. Repeat at the end of four weeks (if maintained) and six weeks after initial date of attainment.

▲ Box in the skill level to be maintained on the child's Class Record of Progress. Note the date the child attained target level of performance (defined by teacher alone or co-planned with parents).

▲ Two weeks after attainment, observe the child. Is the level maintained? If child does not demonstrate the skill components at the desired level of performance, indicate the skill components that need reteaching or reinforcing in the comments sheet on the Class Record of Progress. Reschedule teaching time, and co-plan with parents the home activities necessary to reinforce child's achievement of the skill components and maintenance of attainment.

▲ Continue to observe the child, and reteach and reinforce until the child maintains that level of performance for six weeks.

▲ Plan teaching activities incorporating these components so that the child can continually use and reinforce them and can acquire new ones over the year.

▲ When the child can understand it, make a checklist poster illustrating the child's achievements. Bring the child's attention to these skill components in various compatible play and game activities throughout the year. Have the child help others—a partner or a small group.

In Co-Planning with Parent(s)

1. Encourage the parent(s) to reinforce the child's achievement of the skill components in everyday play and living activities in the home.

▲ Provide key action words for the parent(s) to emphasize.

▲ Give the parent(s) a list of play and games to use in playing with the child, thus reinforcing the skill components the child has achieved and needs support to maintain.

▲ Give the parent(s) a list of activities that can be done at home with the child, such as

    a. Traveling on the scooterboard around the obstacle course (up and down inclines, under table, around chair).

    b. Traveling on the scooterboard "highway" on the playground. Follow the basic traffic safety principles. Use "road map."

    c. Forming a train with friends with the scooterboards while traveling in straight path.

    d. Traveling on the scooterboard around your neighborhood.

2. Set up a time every two weeks to interact with the parent(s) and exchange feedback on the child's progress.

Performance Objective

The child placed on a slide by the teacher can slide three consecutive times, demonstrating the following skill components:

On a playground slide 3 to 10 feet long, the child can

1. slide down 3 feet or more in any manner (sitting, on back, on front) and

2. slide down 3 feet or more, maintaining upright sitting position, holding handrails.

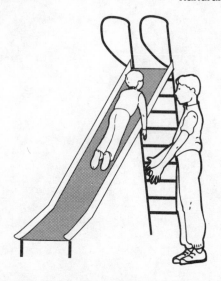 

Action Words

Actions: Climb, go, grip, hold, sit, slide, stop

Objects: Back, belly, feet, hand, leg, rails, seat, side, slide

Concepts: Backward, bottom, down, forward, look, on, ready, show me, top, up

Games

- Do What I Do
- Follow the Ball
- Follow the Leader
- Obstacle Course
- Sliding into the Pool
- Water Slide

TEACHING ACTIVITIES

If a child requires assistance to respond,

1. give verbal cues and physical assistance.
Assist the child by sitting at the top of the slide with child between your legs. Then slide down together. Give child a slight push forward. While child slides down, give specific verbal instructions throughout (in sign language, bliss symbols, action cues), such as "One, two, three, go."

2. give verbal cues with demonstration.
Use model or have the child watch you slide down the slide. Then have the child perform the action. Use specific verbal instructions (as in 1 above with the modeling).

If a child can respond without assistance,

3. give a verbal challenge in the form of a problem: "Who can . . . ?" "Show me how you can . . ."
a. Slide down the slide on your seat.
b. Slide down the slide on your back.
c. Slide down the slide on your stomach.
d. Variation: Slide to music.

4. introduce self-initiated learning activities.
Set up the equipment and space for sliding down a slide. Provide time at the beginning of the lesson and free time for independent learning after the child understands the skills to be used. You may ask the child to create a game activity to play alone or with others (partner or small group) on the equipment.

5. Variations: Set up an obstacle course that includes colored tape to slide on a slide. Play a game, such as Follow the Leader or Follow the Ball, that incorporates sliding down a slide.

Performance Objective

The child with acquisition of Skill Level 1 and the ability to ascend stairs and sit down on slide can slide down sitting three consecutive times, demonstrating the following skill components:

On a playground slide 3 to 10 feet long, the child can

3. assume ready position by sitting upright, grasp handrails with hands, extend legs forward down slide and

4. slide down 3 feet or more in upright position with hands on rails and

5. stop movement at end of slide by touching feet to ground or tightening grasp on rails.

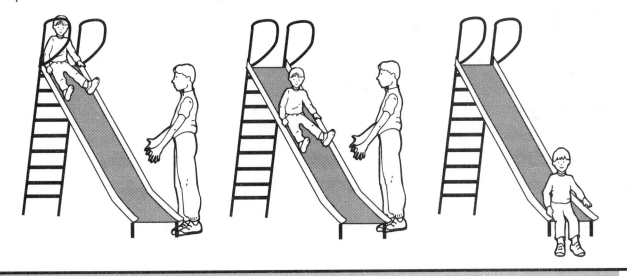

Skills to Review

1. Slide down 3 feet or more in any manner (sitting, on back, on front) and

2. slide down 3 feet or more, maintaining upright sitting position, holding handrails.

Action Words

Actions: Climb, go, grip, hold, sit, slide, stop

Objects: Back, belly, feet, hand, leg, rails, seat, side, slide

Concepts: Backward, bottom, down, forward, look, on, ready, show me, top, up

Games

Do What I Do

Follow the Ball

Follow the Leader

Obstacle Course

Sliding into the Pool

Water Slide

TEACHING ACTIVITIES

If a child requires assistance to respond,

1. give verbal cues and physical assistance.
Assist the child by holding child's waist as he or she sits on slide and slides down. Then have child hold onto side rails with hands and slide. The child should grip side rails tight at end of slide and stop action with feet touching ground. Give the child specific verbal instructions throughout (in sign language, bliss symbols, action cues), such as "Slide down," "Sit on the slide," "One, two, three, go."

2. give verbal cues with demonstration.
Use a model or have the child watch you slide down the slide. Have child do it immediately after it has been demonstrated. Use specific verbal instructions (as in 1 above with the modeling).

If a child can respond without assistance,

3. give a verbal challenge in the form of a problem: "Who can . . . ?" "Show me how you can . . ."

a. Slide down the slide on your seat.

b. Slide down as fast as you can.

c. Slide down as slow as you can.

d. Variation: Slide to music.

4. introduce self-initiated learning activities.
Set up the equipment and space for sliding down a
slide. Provide time at the beginning of the lesson
and free time for independent learning after the
child understands the skills to be used. You may
ask the child to create a game activity to play
alone or with others (partner or small group) on the
equipment.

5. Variations: Set up an obstacle course that
includes colored tape to slide on a slide. Play a
game, such as Follow the Leader or Follow the Ball,
that incorporates sliding down a slide.

SLIDE DOWN A SLIDE: SKILL LEVEL 3

Performance Objective

The child with acquisition of Skill Level 2 or a level of performance appropriate for the child's level of functioning can maintain that level over six weeks.

Given opportunity to use the skill, the child can

1. play two or more games listed below at home or school, and
2. play with equipment selected by teacher and parent(s).

Skills to Review

1. Level 1 sliding. Slide down 3 feet or more in any manner (sitting, on back, on front) and
2. slide down 3 feet or more, maintaining upright sitting position, holding handrails.
3. Level 2 sliding. Assume ready position by grasping handrails with hands, extend legs forward down slide and
4. slide down 3 feet or more in upright position with hands on rails, and
5. stop movement at end of slide by touching feet to ground or tightening grasp on rails.

Action Words

Actions: Climb, go, grip, hold, sit, slide, stop

Objects: Back, belly, feet, hand, leg, rails, seat, side, slide

Concepts: Backward, bottom, down, forward, look, on, ready, show me, top, up

Games

- Do What I Do
- Follow the Ball
- Follow the Leader
- Obstacle Course
- Sliding into the Pool
- Water Slide

TEACHING ACTIVITIES FOR MAINTENANCE

In Teaching

1. Provide the child with teaching cues (verbal and nonverbal, such as demonstration, modeling, imitating) for sliding down a slide that involve the skill components the child has achieved in compatible teaching and play activities. Bring to the child's attention the skill components he or she has already achieved. Provide positive reinforcement and feedback for the child.
2. Use games that require sliding down a slide and that involve imitating, modeling, and demonstrating.
3. Observe and assess each child's maintenance at the end of two weeks. Repeat at the end of four weeks (if maintained) and six weeks after initial date of attainment.
▲ Box in the skill level to be maintained on the child's Class Record of Progress. Note the date the child attained target level of performance (defined by teacher alone or co-planned with parents).
▲ Two weeks after attainment, observe the child. Is the level maintained? If child does not demonstrate the skill components at the desired level of performance, indicate the skill components that need reteaching or reinforcing in the comments sheet on the Class Record of Progress. Reschedule teaching time, and co-plan with parents the home activities necessary to reinforce child's achievement of the skill components and maintenance of attainment.
▲ Continue to observe the child, and reteach and reinforce until the child maintains that level of performance for six weeks.
▲ Plan teaching activities incorporating these components so that the child can continually use and reinforce them and can acquire new ones over the year.

▲ When the child can understand it, make a checklist poster illustrating the child's achievements. Bring the child's attention to these skill components in various compatible play and game activities throughout the year. Have the child help others— a partner or a small group.

In Co-Planning with Parent(s)

1. Encourage the parent(s) to reinforce the child's achievement of the skill components in everyday play and living activities in the home.
▲ Provide key action words for the parent(s) to emphasize.
▲ Give the parent(s) a list of play and games to use in playing with the child, thus reinforcing the skill components the child has achieved and needs support to maintain.
▲ Give the parent(s) a list of activities that can be done at home with the child, such as
   a. Rolling ball down the slide and trying to catch it while sliding down the slide.
   b. Sliding down the slippery wet slide into a swimming pool or at a water slide park.
2. Set up a time every two weeks to interact with the parent(s) and exchange feedback on the child's progress.

Checklists:
Individual and Class Records of Progress

A checklist is an objective score sheet for each play skill taught in the program. By observing and assessing each child's level of performance, you can identify the activities that will assist the child in reaching the performance objective. Use the same checklist to monitor the child's progress during instruction. When the child's performance level changes, you can upgrade the learning tasks (skill components) to the child's skill level.

To Begin

Decide on one or more play skills to be taught in the program. Become familiar with the description of the performance objective for each activity selected. Review the scoring key on the checklist. Plan assessing activities for the selected skills. The number will depend on the class size, the needs of the children, and the help available to you. Set up testing stations similar to the learning stations. Some teachers use free-play time (after setting up equipment for the objective to be tested) to observe the children.

1. Begin assessing at Skill Level 2 for the particular objective. If the child cannot perform at Skill Level 2, assess for Skill Level 1. If the child demonstrates the skill components for Skill Level 2 (i.e., with modeling, verbal cues, or no cues), the child has achieved functional competence. At the next skill level, Skill Level 3, the child demonstrates maintenance retention of the skill over time.

2. For some children with special needs, you may need to assess their levels of functioning before planning teaching activities. As in step 1, observe and assess the amount and type of assistance (cues) the child needs in descending order (i.e., from verbal cues to total manipulation).

Code	Amount and Type of Assistance
SI	Child initiates demonstrating the skill in the teaching and playing of activities
C	Child demonstrates the skill when given verbal cues with or without demonstration
A	Child demonstrates the skill when given partial assistance or total manipulation throughout the execution of the skill

Record, using the code above, the child's initial assistance level and progress in the comments column of the Class Record of Progress. For some children, this may be the most significant initial progress noted (i.e., from assistance to verbal cues and demonstration).

To Assess

1. Be sure all children are working on objectives at other stations while you are assessing at one station.

2. Make sure there is enough space for the skill to be tested.

3. For swinging on a swing, have three or four children (depending on the number of swings) get on a swing. Each child takes a turn on the command "go." At the end of the trials, record each child's performance on the score sheet.

4. For hanging from a bar and sliding down a slide, have three or four children line up next to equipment. One by one, each child takes a turn on the equipment. At the end of the trials, record each child's performance on the score sheet.

5. For pushing and pulling an object, riding a tricycle or bicycle, and traveling on a scooterboard, have three or four children stand on a line. On the command "go," each child takes a turn performing the requested skill. At the end of the trials, record each child's performance on the score sheet.

6. You may need to modify the assessing activity by taking a child through the pattern or modeling the activity and using sign language or an interpreter. Other modifications are individual assessment or free play with the equipment. Use mats or movable walls to cut down on distractions.

To Adapt the Checklists

You can note children's skill components adaptations (i.e., physical devices or other changes) in the comments column on the Class Record of Progress. Other changes can be written under recommendations for individual children or the class. Modifications made for a child can be noted on the Individual Record of Progress. The Class Record of Progress can be adapted for an individual child. Record the name of the child rather than the class, and in the name column, record assessment dates. This adaptation may be needed for children whose progress is erratic, because it provides a baseline assessment to find out where to begin teaching and evaluating the child's progress.

The Individual Record of Progress for the end-of-the-year report can be attached to the child's IEP (Individual Education Program) report. The record can also serve as a cumulative record for each child. Such records are very useful for new teachers, substitute teachers, aides, and volunteers, as well as parents. The format of the Individual Record of Progress can also be adapted for a Unit Report. The names of all the objectives for a

unit—for example, walk-run endurance, running, catching a ball, and rolling a ball—are written rather than the names of the children. Book 8 illustrates the adaptation of the Individual Record of Progress for use in the Home Activities Program and for a Unit Report.

The checklists may be reproduced as needed to implement the play and motor skills program.

CLASS RECORD OF PROGRESS REPORT

CLASS _____   DATE _____

AGE/GRADE _____   TEACHER _____

SCHOOL _____

OBJECTIVE: HANG FROM A BAR

SCORING:	SKILL LEVEL 1		SKILL LEVEL 2	SKILL LEVEL 3	PRIMARY RESPONSES:
ASSESSMENT:	Three Consecutive Times				N = Not Attending
_____Date					NR = No Response
X = Achieved					UR = Unrelated Response
O = Not Achieved					O = Other (Specify in comments)
/ = Partially Achieved					
REASSESSMENT:	Reaches up and grasps bar with hands, feet off ground, and hangs for 5 seconds.	With hands and knees, hangs for 5 seconds.	Releases hands and hangs with knees for 5 seconds.	Two or more play or game activities at home or school demonstrating skill components over six-week period.	
_____Date					
⊗ = Achieved					
Ø = Not Achieved					
NAME	1	2	3	4	COMMENTS
1.					
2.					
3.					
4.					
5.					
6.					
7.					
8.					
9.					
10.					

Recommendations: Specific changes or conditions in planning for instructions, performance, or diagnostic testing procedures or standards. Please describe what worked best.

_____

_____

_____

_____

_____

CLASS RECORD OF PROGRESS REPORT

CLASS _____   DATE _____

AGE/GRADE _____   TEACHER _____

SCHOOL _____

OBJECTIVE: PUSH AND PULL AN OBJECT

SCORING:	SKILL LEVEL 1		SKILL LEVEL 2			SKILL LEVEL 3	PRIMARY RESPONSES:
ASSESSMENT: _____Date	Three Consecutive Times						N = Not Attending
X = Achieved							NR = No Response
O = Not Achieved							UR = Unrelated Response
/ = Partially Achieved							O = Other (Specify in comments)
REASSESSMENT: _____Date	While moving forward, pushes an object with two hands for 10 feet.	While moving forward, pushes an object with two hands around three obstacles 5 feet apart without bumping obstacles.	While moving backward, pulls an object with one or two hands for 10 feet.	While moving forward, pulls an object with one or two hands for 10 feet.	Pulls an object with one or two hands around three obstacles 5 feet apart without bumping obstacles.	Two or more play or game activities at home or school demonstrating skill components over six-week period.	
⊗ = Achieved							
Ø = Not Achieved							
NAME	1	2	3	4	5	6	COMMENTS
1.							
2.							
3.							
4.							
5.							
6.							
7.							
8.							
9.							
10.							

Recommendations: Specific changes or conditions in planning for instructions, performance, or diagnostic testing procedures or standards. Please describe what worked best.

_____

_____

_____

_____

_____

Class Record of Progress Report

CLASS _____ DATE _____

AGE/GRADE _____ TEACHER _____

SCHOOL _____

OBJECTIVE: RIDE A TRICYCLE OR BICYCLE

SCORING:	SKILL LEVEL 1		SKILL LEVEL 2		SKILL LEVEL 3	PRIMARY RESPONSES:
ASSESSMENT: _____Date **X** = Achieved **O** = Not Achieved / = Partially Achieved REASSESSMENT: _____Date Ⓧ = Achieved Ø = Not Achieved	Three Consecutive Times					N = Not Attending NR = No Response UR = Unrelated Response O = Other (Specify in comments)
	Sits on bike and grasps handlebars, with feet maintaining contact on pedals, and is pushed 10 feet or more.	Sits on bike and grasps handlebars, with feet maintaining contact on pedals, and pushes down with right foot on up pedal, pushes down with left foot on up pedal, riding 10 feet or more.	Sits on bike and grasps handlebars, with feet on pedals in up position, and pushes down with right foot, then pushes down with left foot, riding a distance of 20 feet or more.	Sits on bike and grasps handlebars, with feet on pedals, and rides the bike around three obstacles aligned 10 feet apart without bumping obstacles.	Two or more play or game activities at home or school demonstrating skill components over six-week period.	
NAME	1	2	3	4	5	COMMENTS
1.						
2.						
3.						
4.						
5.						
6.						
7.						
8.						
9.						
10.						

Recommendations: Specific changes or conditions in planning for instructions, performance, or diagnostic testing procedures or standards. Please describe what worked best.

_____

_____

_____

_____

_____

CLASS RECORD OF PROGRESS REPORT

CLASS _____ DATE _____

AGE/GRADE _____ TEACHER _____

SCHOOL _____

OBJECTIVE: SWING ON A SWING

	SKILL LEVEL 1		SKILL LEVEL 2		SKILL LEVEL 3	
SCORING: ASSESSMENT: _____Date **X** = Achieved **O** = Not Achieved **/** = Partially Achieved REASSESSMENT: _____Date ⊗ = Achieved ∅ = Not Achieved	Three Consecutive Times					**PRIMARY RESPONSES:** N = Not Attending NR = No Response UR = Unrelated Response O = Other (Specify in comments)
	Sits and is pushed in 4- to 6-foot arc for five or more pushes.	Pushing with feet against ground, initiates swinging in 2- to 4-foot arc for three cycles (forward and backward).	Leans back, extending legs, as swing moves forward, and leans forward, bending knees, as swing moves backward in 2- to 4-foot arc for five cycles.	Swings forward and backward in 4- to 6-foot arc for ten cycles.	Two or more play or game activities at home or school demonstrating skill components over six-week period.	
NAME	1	2	3	4	5	COMMENTS
1.						
2.						
3.						
4.						
5.						
6.						
7.						
8.						
9.						
10.						

Recommendations: Specific changes or conditions in planning for instructions, performance, or diagnostic testing procedures or standards. Please describe what worked best.

_____

_____

_____

_____

_____

CLASS RECORD OF PROGRESS REPORT

CLASS _____   DATE _____

AGE/GRADE _____   TEACHER _____

SCHOOL _____

OBJECTIVE: TRAVEL ON A SCOOTERBOARD

NAME	SKILL LEVEL 1 — Three Consecutive Times — Assumes ready position on scooterboard and is pushed without falling off for 10 feet or more.	SKILL LEVEL 1 — Three Consecutive Times — Assumes ready position on a scooterboard and pushes with hands or feet, traveling 5 feet or more in any direction.	SKILL LEVEL 2 — Travels on scooterboard in a 5-foot-wide path for 15 or more feet.	SKILL LEVEL 2 — Travels on scooterboard around three obstacles aligned 5 feet apart without bumping obstacles.	SKILL LEVEL 3 — Two or more play or game activities at home or school demonstrating skill components over six-week period.	COMMENTS
	1	2	3	4	5	
1.						
2.						
3.						
4.						
5.						
6.						
7.						
8.						
9.						
10.						

Recommendations: Specific changes or conditions in planning for instructions, performance, or diagnostic testing procedures or standards. Please describe what worked best.

_____

_____

_____

_____

_____

CLASS RECORD OF PROGRESS REPORT

CLASS _____ DATE _____

AGE/GRADE _____ TEACHER _____

SCHOOL _____

OBJECTIVE: SLIDE DOWN A SLIDE

SCORING:	SKILL LEVEL 1		SKILL LEVEL 2			SKILL LEVEL 3	PRIMARY RESPONSES:
ASSESSMENT: ____Date **X** = Achieved **O** = Not Achieved / = Partially Achieved REASSESSMENT: ____Date ⊗ = Achieved Ø = Not Achieved	Three Consecutive Times						N = Not Attending NR = No Response UR = Unrelated Response O = Other (Specify in comments)
	Slides down 3 feet or more in any manner (sitting, on back, on front).	Slides down 3 feet or more, maintaining upright sitting position, holding handrails.	Assumes ready position by grasping handrails with hands, extends legs forward down slide.	Slides down 3 feet or more in upright position, with hands on rails.	Stops movement at end of slide by touching feet to ground or tightening grasp on rails.	Two or more play or game activities at home or school demonstrating skill components over six-week period.	
NAME	1	2	3	4	5	6	COMMENTS
1.							
2.							
3.							
4.							
5.							
6.							
7.							
8.							
9.							
10.							

Recommendations: Specific changes or conditions in planning for instructions, performance, or diagnostic testing procedures or standards. Please describe what worked best.

_____

_____

_____

_____

_____

INDIVIDUAL RECORD OF PROGRESS

Area: Play Skills

CHILD: _____

	Marking Period	*Date*
LEVEL: _____	Fall Conference (white)	from____to____
YEAR: _____	Winter Conference (yellow)	from____to____
TEACHER: _____	Spring Conference (pink)	from____to____
SCHOOL: _____	End-of-Year (cumulative) Report (blue)	from____to____

Preprimary Play and Motor Skills Activity Program

The Individual Record of Progress lists all of the objectives in which your child receives instruction during the play and motor skills program. The information reported on your child's Individual Record of Progress shows your child's entry performance and progress for a marking period. The end-of-the-year report represents your child's Individual Education Program (IEP) for the objectives selected and taught during the year.

Each objective is broken into small, measurable steps or skill components. This assists the teacher to assess what your child already knew before teaching began and to determine which step to start teaching first. One of the following symbols is marked by each step or skill component of the objective:

X = The child already knew how to perform this step before teaching it began.

O = The child did not know how to perform this step before teaching it began or after instruction of it ended.

⊘ = The child did not know how to perform this step before teaching it began, but did learn how to do it during the instruction period.

This information should be helpful to you in planning home activities to strengthen your child's play and motor skills.

Comments

_____

_____

_____

_____

_____

_____

_____

_____

HANG FROM A BAR

Date: _____

From a bar adjusted to shoulder height
Three consecutive times

—— Reaches up and grasps bar with hands, feet off ground, and hangs for 5 seconds.

—— With hands and knees, hangs for 5 seconds.

—— Releases hands and hangs with knees for 5 seconds.

—— Demonstrates above skill in two or more play or game activities at home or school over a six-week period.

PUSH AND PULL AN OBJECT

Date: _____

Within a clear space of 20 feet
Three consecutive times

—— While moving forward, pushes an object with two hands for 10 feet.

—— While moving forward, pushes an object with two hands around three obstacles 5 feet apart without bumping obstacles.

—— While moving backward, pulls an object with one or two hands for 10 feet.

—— While moving forward, pulls an object with one or two hands for 10 feet.

—— Pulls an object with one or two hands around three obstacles 5 feet apart without bumping obstacles.

—— Demonstrates above skill in two or more play or game activities at home or school over a six-week period.

RIDE A TRICYCLE OR BICYCLE

Date: _____

Within a clear space of 30 feet
Three consecutive times

—— Assumes ready position by sitting on bike and grasping handlebars, with feet maintaining contact on pedals, and is pushed 10 feet or more.

—— Assumes ready position by sitting on bike and grasping handlebars, with feet maintaining contact on pedals, and pushes down with right foot on up pedal, pushes down with left foot on up pedal, riding 10 feet or more.

—— Assumes ready position by sitting on bike and grasping handlebars, with feet pedals in up position, pushes down with right foot, then pushes down with left foot, riding a distance of 20 feet or more.

—— Assumes ready position by sitting on bike and grasping handlebars, with feet on pedals, and rides the bike around three obstacles aligned 10 feet apart without bumping obstacles.

—— Demonstrates above skill in two or more play or game activities at home or school over a six-week period.

SWING ON A SWING

Date: _____

On a swing adjusted so that child's feet touch ground

____ Sits and is pushed in 4- to 6-foot arc for five or more pushes.

____ Pushing with feet against ground, initiates swinging in 2- to 4-foot arc for three cycles (forward and backward).

____ Leans back, extending legs, as swing moves forward, and leans forward, bending knees, as swing moves backward in 2- to 4-foot arc for five cycles.

____ Swings forward and backward in 4- to 6-foot arc for ten cycles.

____ Demonstrates above skill in two or more play or game activities at home or school over a six-week period.

TRAVEL ON A SCOOTERBOARD

Date: _____

Within a clear space of 30 feet

____ Assumes ready position on scooterboard and is pushed without falling off for 10 feet or more.

____ Assumes ready position on scooterboard and pushes with hands or feet, traveling 5 feet or more in any direction.

____ Travels on scooterboard in a 5-foot-wide path for 15 or more feet.

____ Travels on scooterboard around three obstacles aligned 5 feet apart without bumping obstacles.

____ Demonstrates above skill in two or more play or game activities at home or school over a six-week period.

SLIDE DOWN A SLIDE

Date: _____

On a slide 3 to 10 feet long

____ Slides down 3 feet or more in any manner (sitting, on back, on front).

____ Slides down 3 feet or more, maintaining upright sitting position, holding handrails.

____ Assumes ready position by grasping handrails with hands, extends legs forward down slide.

____ Slides down 3 feet or more in upright position with hands on rails.

____ Stops movement at end of slide by touching feet to ground or tightening grasp on rails.

____ Demonstrates above skill in two or more play or game activities at home or school over a six-week period.

Games

Game Selection

The following game sheets will help you select and plan game activities. They include the names of the games in alphabetical order, formation, directions, equipment, play skills, and type of play activity. Consider the following points when selecting games:

1. Skills and objectives of your program
2. Interest of the child
3. Equipment and rules
4. Adaptability of physical difficulty level in order to match each child's ability
5. Activity for healthy growth and development
6. Social play skill development, such as taking turns, sharing equipment, playing with others, and following and leading

Games can foster creativity. Children enjoy making up, interpreting, and creating their own activities, whether playing alone, with a partner, or with a small group. The time you take to provide opportunities for each child to explore and create will be well spent. One further note. Children can easily create or adapt games matched to their mobility, even if limited by crutches, braces, or wheelchairs. Play skills activities involve moving from here to there. These children easily comprehend how to get to "there" with their own expertise for movement.

Following are some suggestions for adapting the physical difficulty level of games and a sequential list of social play development.

Adapting Games

To Change	Use	Example
1. Boundaries	Larger or smaller space	Make bases 10 feet apart or 20 feet apart for Base Running game on tricycles or bicycles.
2. Equipment	Larger or smaller sizes, weights, or heights, or specially adapted equipment for some children (such as guide-rails, inclines rather than stairs, brightly colored mats)	Swing on chair swings or bucket-seat swings.

3. Rules	More or fewer rules	In Hot Rods on bikes, change direction of movement from clockwise to counterclockwise.
4. Actions	More or fewer actions to be performed at one time; play in stationary positions, using various body parts	Slide down slide on one, two, or three body parts.
5. Time of play	Longer or shorter time; frequent rest periods	In Tug of War, pull rope for 2 minutes, then 5 minutes.

To adapt games to other special needs, you might also use buddies and spotters, sign language gestures, or place the child near leader.

Sequential Development of Social Play

Sequence	*Description*	*Example of Play Activity*
Individual Play	Child plays alone and independently with toys that are different from those used by other children within speaking distance.	Child rides tricycle on pavement while other children play with balls, ropes, etc.
Parallel Play	Child plays independently beside, rather than with, other children.	Child plays on scooterboard. Other children also play on scooterboards. No interaction between children.
Associate Play	Child plays with other children. There is interaction between children, but there are no common goals.	Child plays Fishing independently alongside other children.
Cooperative Play	Child plays within a group organized for playing formal games. Group is goal directed.	Children play Cageball Push together.

Game Sheet Lesson Plans

Games	Organization	Description/Instructions	Equipment	Skills	Type of Play Activity
Balloon Push	Line 	Seat children in two rows, with legs 1 foot away from center line. Toss balloon up over center line. Have children use any body part to push balloon over line to children on other side. Can sit or stand and use broom.	Inflated balloon or beach ball; broom (optional)	Push and pull	Small group, large group
Base Running	Circle 	Each child sits on a bike or scooterboard by a base. Children bike around bases. At signal, all stop by base nearest them.	Bases or carpet squares; drum; whistle; tricycles, bicycles, or scooterboards	Tricycle or bike riding, travel on a scooterboard	Relay; small group, large group
Bike Relay	Lines 	Have children line up in two lines. On signal, first child travels around traffic cones on bike and then back to the line. Gives bike to next person in line and goes to end of line.	Traffic cones; bikes	Tricycle or bike riding	Relay; partner, small group, large group
Cageball Push	Line 	Each child in turn pushes cageball with both hands over goal line and back to start.	Cageball	Push	Relay; individual, partners, small group, large group

GAME SHEET LESSON PLANS

Games	Organization	Description/Instructions	Equipment	Skills	Type of Play Activity
Circle Strike Ball	Circle	Children sit on scooterboards, with hockey sticks. Toss ball into circle. Children travel on scooterboards and try to strike ball outside of circle boundaries.	Ball; hockey sticks; scooterboards	Travel on a scooterboard	Small group, large group
Crossing the Lake	Circle	When music starts, all children bike around circle. When music stops, any child caught in lake must drop out.	Tape or chalk; ropes; drums or record player; tricycles or bikes, scooterboards	Tricycle or bike riding, travel on scooterboard	Small group, large group
Did You Ever See a Lassie/Laddie?	Line / Semicircle	Leader starts song, performs activity. Children mimic movements.	All play equipment	All play skills	Partners, small group
Do What I Do	Line	Children stand in line behind leader or near slide. Imitate movements of leader. Climb on slide, sit down, slide.	Slide	Slide	Partners, small group, large group

Game Sheet Lesson Plans

Games	Organization	Description/Instructions	Equipment	Skills	Type of Play Activity
Do This, Do That	Circle	Leader demonstrates movement. Children imitate leader on "do this."	All play equipment	All play skills	Small group, large group
Follow the Ball	Line	Children line up behind leader. Roll a ball down the slide and slide down after it. Try to catch it before it hits the bottom.	Slide	Slide	Individual, partners, small group, large group
Follow the Leader	Line	Demonstrate various actions and have children imitate. Choose different leaders.	All play skills	All play skills	Small group, large group
Freeze	Line or circle	Children ride a tricycle, bike, or scooter. They "freeze" when the signal to stop is given.	Scooterboard, bikes	Tricycle or bike riding, travel on a scooter	Small group, large group

GAME SHEET LESSON PLANS

GAMES	ORGANIZATION	DESCRIPTION/INSTRUCTIONS	EQUIPMENT	SKILLS	TYPE OF PLAY ACTIVITY
Giants and Dragons	Line Dragons X X X X Giants X X X X	Divide group in half, with each group behind a line 15–20 feet apart. On signal, giants ride toward dragons' cave, and dragons get ready to chase. When giants are very close, teacher signals, "Dragons are coming," and giants ride home. If tagged, they become dragons.	Tape to mark lines; tricycles or bikes; scooterboards	Tricycle or bike riding, travel on a scooterboard	Tag; small group, large group
Hill Dill	x x x x x taggers x x x x x	Begin with one tagger. He or she says, "Hill Dill come over the hill." If you are tagged, you help tagger get others.	Tricycle or bikes, scooterboards	Tricycle or bike riding, travel on a scooterboard	Tag; small group, large group
Hot Rods	pit stop	When teacher says "go," hot rods ride two times around gym on blue line. When done, sit in pit stop.	Blue tape to make track; tricycles or bikes, scooterboards	Tricycle or bike riding, travel on a scooterboard	Tag; small group, large group
How High Can You Fly?	Line X X X X X X X X X	Children line up in back of swings. Say, "Try to swing as high as you can. Like a bird in the sky, how high can you fly?"	Swing	Swing	Relay; individual, partners, small group, large group

GAME SHEET LESSON PLANS

GAMES	ORGANIZATION	DESCRIPTION/INSTRUCTIONS	EQUIPMENT	SKILLS	TYPE OF PLAY ACTIVITY
Jet Pilots	XXXXX (arrows)	Teacher is starter. Says, "Jet pilots take off, ride to other line." First one to other side is new starter.	Tricycles or bikes, scooterboards	Tricycle or bike riding, travel on a scooterboard	Relay; small group, large group
Modified Shuffleboard	Line X X X → ○ X X X ↓ ○	Push beanbag with the stick to the circle. Push it back to next person in line.	Beanbag, stick	Push	Individual, small group, large group
Monkey-Bar Hang Relay	Line X X X (arrows to bars) X X X	Have child from each team run to monkey bars, hang as long as he or she can, and then run back to end of line.	Monkey bars, horizontal bars, parallel bars	Hang	Relay; small group, large group
Pushbroom	Line X X X X →	Children in turn push small ball over goal line and back to start.	Brooms; 8"–10" ball	Push	Relay; individual, partners, small group, large group

Game Sheet Lesson Plans

Games	Organization	Description/Instructions	Equipment	Skills	Type of Play Activity
Pushing a Box as a Group	Scatter	Children assist by pushing boxes of materials to site.	Large cardboard boxes	Push	Small group, large group
Sandbox Relay	Scatter	Children push and pull cars and trucks through sand, and shovel sand into cars and trucks. Have children push twigs into sand to make trees in sand valleys, and push and pull shovel through sand to make roads.	Sandbox; trucks, cars; shovels, pails	Push and pull	Small group, large group
Scooterboard Races	Lines	Children line up in two lines. On signal, they travel around traffic cones on scooterboards and back to the line. Give scooterboard to next person in line and go to end of line.	2 traffic cones; scooterboard	Travel on a scooter-board	Relay; partner, small group, large group
Simon Says	Line or circle	Demonstrate various play skills. Child imitates on command "Simon says (do this)." Have children imitate actions only on hearing "Simon says."	All play equipment	All play skills	Small group, large group

GAME SHEET LESSON PLANS

GAMES	ORGANIZATION	DESCRIPTION/INSTRUCTIONS	EQUIPMENT	SKILLS	TYPE OF PLAY ACTIVITY
Sliding into the Pool	Line	Children line up and one by one climb stairs and slide down into swimming pool.	Slide; swimming pool	Slide	Individual, partners, small group, large group
Tug of War	Lines	Divide children in half. Have each group grab hold of one end of rope. Encourage each group to pull hard to bring other group over line.	Long, sturdy rope	Pull	Small group, large group
Water Slide	Line	Hose the slide down with water. Have children slide down slide to cool off. (Use only with strict supervision and in school situations where appropriate.)	Slide	Slide	Partners, small group, large group